Royal Family Library

Prince Charles

Purnell

Introduction

HRH Prince Charles Philip Arthur George, eldest son and heir of Her Majesty Queen Elizabeth II and Prince Philip, was born at Buckingham Palace in London on 14th November 1948. When news of his birth became known, there was great rejoicing in the city and the floodlights in Trafalgar Square turned to blue indicating that the child was a prince. After living for a few months at Buckingham Palace, the family moved to Clarence House and the young Prince was often to be seen in nearby parks with his nanny. So life began for the twenty-first Prince of Wales.

His sister, Princess Anne, was born in 1950. A year later, at the age of three, Charles made one of his first public appearances when he went to meet his parents on their return from overseas. He was staying at Sandringham with his grandparents when King George VI died, and his mother returned from Kenya to become Queen of England. From that moment the young Prince's life changed because he was next in line to the throne.

The Royal Family then moved back into Buckingham Palace. With about six hundred rooms and long corridors, it was a splendid playground for Charles. He was four when he was taken to Westminster Abbey to watch his mother's coronation. Gradually, he attended more and more official ceremonies.

Breaking with royal tradition, the prince was not educated privately, but went to a day school in London, a preparatory school in Berkshire and then to his father's old public school, Gordonstoun in Scotland.

The pattern of his life became established and he began playing a more serious role in public life. While at school, he came to London to attend the State funeral of Sir Winston Churchill in January 1965, and in June that year his first public engagement was to attend a garden party for six hundred students at the Palace of Holyroodhouse.

His education continued with six months at Geelong Grammar School in Victoria, Australia, and when he was eighteen he went to Trinity College, Cambridge, spending one term at Aberystwyth University before his Investiture in July 1969.

Prince Charles entered Dartmouth, serving for five years with the Royal Navy, and took a short course at RAF Cranwell. On the 11th February 1970 he took his seat in the House of Lords, and in April that year was sworn in as a Member of the Privy Council. He joined his parents on a tour of New Zealand and Australia to celebrate the bicentennial of the voyage of Captain Cook. In Wellington, the Queen went on the first of her many 'walkabouts', meeting and talking with people in the crowds. Prince Charles was quick to follow her example and became a very popular figure – especially with the girls!

The Prince has undertaken many royal tours and other public duties, all with the same charm and ease of manner, for which he has come to be known. In addition to being Prince of Wales, he is also Duke of Cornwall and takes this office very seriously, attending meetings of the Council and visiting all parts of his Duchy.

He has a spontaneous sense of humour and greatly admires the famous team of comedians, the Goons. When he met them at the Eccentrics Club in 1973 he admitted: 'sparring with them is something I have wanted all my life'. Like the Queen, he is also adept at mimicry.

Charles joined Princess Anne on a two week photographic safari in Kenya in 1971 when she was helping to make a *Blue Peter* children's television film for the Save the Children Fund. The day he visited the site of the jungle hotel Treetops Lodge, it was exactly nineteen years after his mother had heard she was Queen. The original lodge had been destroyed by fire.

The same year, Prince Charles was awarded the Freedom of the City of London and appointed Colonel-in-Chief of a number of regiments, including the Royal Regiment of Wales and the Welsh Guards.

'Life in the Royal Navy is a marvellous training for any future king,' said his great-uncle, the late Lord Louis Mountbatten, to his grandfather. The former Viceroy always watched Prince Charles' progress with a keen interest.

In 1974, the Prince accepted the gift of seventeenth-century Chevening House in Kent, left to him by Lord Stanhope.

On her twenty-first birthday, Queen Elizabeth II gave a speech dedicating her whole life to the service of her country and Prince Charles is following her example. He is an adventurous man, dedicated to the task that awaits him; he has a determination to learn as much as possible about the kingdom he will head and about the people who will be his subjects. He is a participator rather than an observer, and does not baulk at any task however hazardous or unpleasant it may be.

With his wide range of skills, Prince Charles has earned respect from all walks of life, but he still retains the great modesty, wit and charm which endear him to his family and all who are lucky enough to meet him.

His motto, *Ich Dien* (I serve), could not be more fitting, for already he has proved his willingness and ability to do just that and has shown that he is a man conscious of his destiny.

Time will show how well he has learned the lessons of his upbringing and heeded the advice passed on to him from his predecessors.

Early Days

Prince Charles had to learn a hard lesson very early in his life – that because he had been born at Buckingham Palace and was a member of the Royal Family he was different from other children. There was nothing he could do to change this, but it was not easy for him to accept in his early years. After lessons with a governess, he went to the day school, Hill House in Knightsbridge, but two terms later was sent as a boarder to his father's old prep school, Cheam. While he was there, in 1958, the Queen announced that he was to be Prince of Wales. In 1962, just before his fourteenth birthday he went to Gordonstoun Public School in Scotland, as his father had done.

Gordonstoun offered a rigorous existence with no luxury, and the Prince quickly learned how to look after himself. In his last year he played the lead role in a school production of *Macbeth*, passed his A-levels and gained his Duke of Edinburgh Award, and was Guardian (Head Boy). He spent two terms on an exchange visit to Geelong Grammar School at Timbertop, Australia in 1966, and in October 1967 went to Trinity College, Cambridge. He began by reading archaeology, but changed to history and gained his degree. In 1969 he took one term off from study at Trinity to go to Aberystwyth University and improve his knowledge of the Welsh people and language. His education completed, the Prince prepared to embark on a service career.

Left *Prince Charles as a baby in the arms of his mother, then Princess Elizabeth, after his Christening at Buckingham Palace on 15th December 1948. His robe was designed by Prince Albert for Queen Victoria's first-born. This picture, which spans four generations, also shows his great-grandmother, Queen Mary and his grandfather, King George VI. The Palace Chapel had been wrecked by German bombs in World War II, so the service was held in the Music Room. The Lily Font was brought from Windsor for the occasion.*
Opposite above left *Warmly dressed for an outing, Charles rests a hand on his pram cover which is decorated with flag and sailor motifs.*
Opposite above right *Well away from earshot, near the vegetable patch, Prince Charles takes great delight in experimenting with a toy trumpet.*
Opposite below *The late Lord Louis Mountbatten, then Commander-in-Chief at Malta, entertains his great-nephew on one of the island's sunny beaches. His sister and the late Countess Mountbatten look on. The children were on their way to join their parents at Tobruk, where they were piped aboard the royal yacht* Britannia *after a separation of six months.*

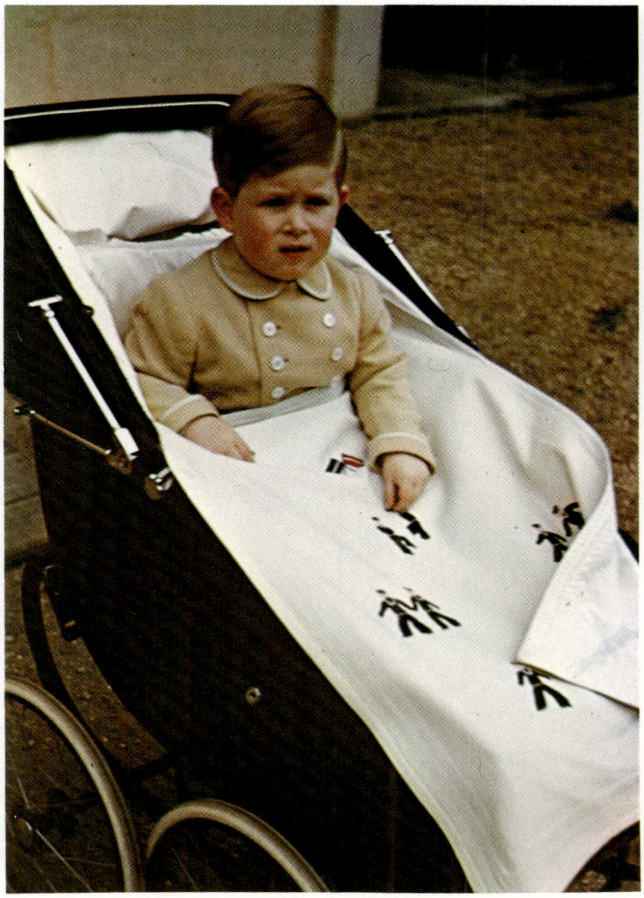

Opposite above left *The five-and-a-half year old Prince rides a pony on a visit to Pets' Corner at London Zoo.*
Opposite above right *Prince Charles at Hill House School Sports Day.*
Opposite below left *Sandringham Flower Show in 1959 provided an early opportunity for Prince Charles to learn the importance of shaking hands as a royal duty.*
Top *Accompanied by his father, the Prince boards a Heron of the Queen's flight for his flight to Gordonstoun.*
Above *One for the boundary!*
Opposite below right *A rare moment of relaxation. The Prince takes a break.*
Left *Prince Charles at his desk dealing with his daily correspondence.*

Opposite *A keen sailor, the Prince began at an early age to learn respect for the sea and to enjoy the delights of sailing.*
Right *The young Prince and his sister, Princess Anne, get a better view at the Badminton Horse Trials by using their binoculars.*
Below *The Prince becoming acquainted with some of his fellow students at Timbertop in Australia, where he spent six months.*
Below right *Here, pouring out his own water ration, he was able to enjoy the novelty of life in the Australian bush as well as the more ordinary scholastic pursuits.*

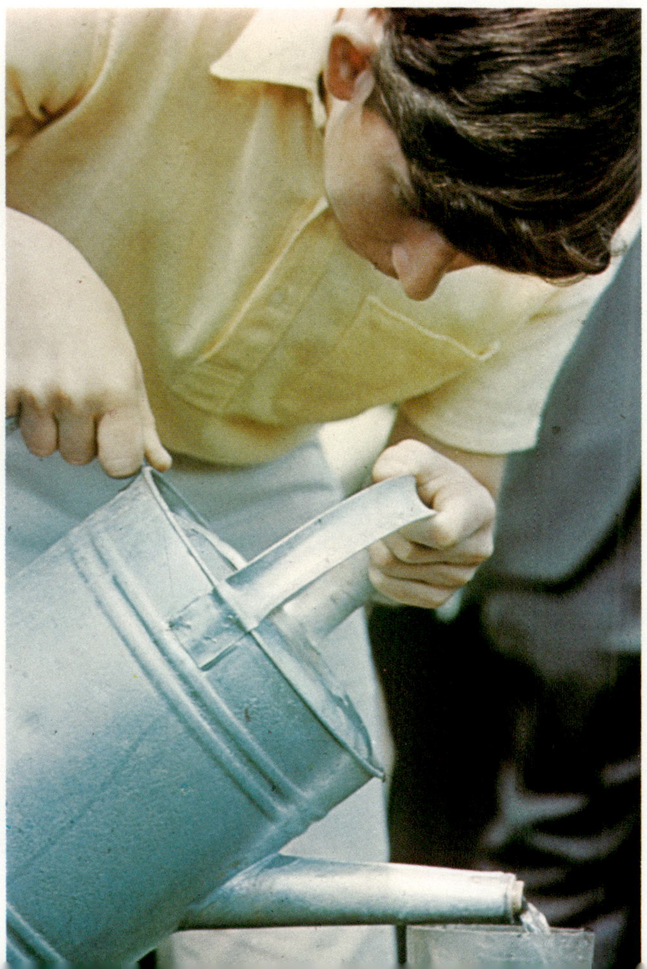

Below *A delightful portrait of Prince Charles taken on his eighteenth birthday. The photograph was taken in the library at Balmoral Castle.*
Opposite *The Prince took part in a Cambridge University revue called* Revolution. *Here, dressed as a Cockney dustman, he delighted the audience with his imitation of his favourite comedians – the Goons.*
Opposite above right *Prince Charles as a student at Trinity College, Cambridge, preparing a snack for himself.*
Opposite below right *For one term, in 1969, Prince Charles went to the University College of Wales at Aberystwyth. This was immediately preceding his Investiture. The language laboratory helped him to become fluent in Welsh.*

GBM

B4

Life in the Services

It was the Prince's wish that he should follow his father, grandfather and great-grandfather and serve in the Royal Navy. He entered the Royal Naval College, Dartmouth at the start of his five years' service in 1971. He had already qualified for a pilot's licence in Cambridge at the age of twenty-one, and obtained his wings as a jet-pilot after a short course at Royal Air Force College, Cranwell. He made history by being the first heir-apparent to make a parachute jump, landing smoothly in the sea near Poole.

While in the Royal Navy, Prince Charles took a three months' course as a helicopter pilot at the Royal Naval Air Station at Yeovilton, and was awarded the double diamond trophy as 'the student who made the most progress'. He has a very keen interest in flying and proved his natural ability by completing one hundred and five flying hours in forty-five days. He also took a tough commando support training course with the Royal Marines at Lympstone and was posted as a naval pilot to the commando carrier HMS *Hermes*. In the Arctic he walked upside-down on ice at the Undersea Research Centre.

In February 1976, Prince Charles was appointed to his first command of a mine-hunter, called HMS *Bronington* at Rosyth. While he was in the Royal Navy the Prince accepted no pay for himself, all monies being donated to the King George's Fund for Sailors.

Opposite *While at Cambridge University, the Prince spent much of his leisure time learning to fly with the RAF at Oakington. One of his instructors was Squadron Leader Philip Pinney. Here he is seen teaching the Prince about the engine.*
Below *In the company of his instructor, the Prince walks towards an RAF Chipmunk trainer aircraft. After fourteen hours of instruction, he made his first solo flight. The ground crew presented him with a model of a Chipmunk after he attained his flying badge.*

Right *Prince Charles was awarded his wings at the annual passing out parade of RAF College, Cranwell. He had passed the Advanced Flying Course and was now qualified to fly jet-fighters. The wings were presented by Air Chief Marshal Sir Dennis Spotswood, Chief of the Air Staff. The Prince's grandfather, King George VI, was the first member of the Royal family to fly with the RAF.*

Below and Opposite above *As part of his training with the Royal Navy, the Prince took a course in helicopter flying. In 1975, at the Royal Naval Air Station, Yeovilton in Somerset, the Prince prepares to board his first helicopter. Prince Philip is also a qualified helicopter pilot, and often flies his own machine, landing it on the lawns of Buckingham Palace.*

Opposite below *The Prince checks the controls before take-off in his helicopter.*

WA
ROYAL NAVY

MAP CASE
OPEN

BRONINGTON

Opposite above *The Prince took command of HMS* Bronington *in Rosyth in February 1976. The ship, appropriately named after a Welsh village, was small, about 365 tonnes. The ship's crew consisted of five officers and thirty-four men. Here the bearded Prince is seen with some of them.*
Opposite below *HMS* Bronington's *role during the Prince's tour of duty was to patrol the shipping lanes of the North Sea and the Channel. It was rough sailing and the captain was often seasick!*
Above *As Colonel-in-Chief of the Royal Regiment of Wales, the Prince takes his duties seriously. He visited his men at Osnabruck in West Germany, learning of their conditions at first-hand. A great believer in finding out for himself, the Prince discovers how hot and uncomfortable a tank can be from the inside.*
Left *Inspecting men on exercise, the Prince stops to chat informally.*

These two portraits of Prince Charles and Princess Anne were commissioned by the Royal Naval College Greenwich and painted by Bernard Hailstone. Princess Anne is wearing the uniform of Chief Commandant of the WRNS. On 1st July 1974, she succeeded the late Princess Marina who held the appointment during the Second World War.

Below left *Prince Charles complete with sword in the uniform of a Commander RN.*
Below right *In full dress uniform as Colonel-in-Chief of the Gordon Highlanders.*
Opposite above left *In service dress of the Royal Regiment of Wales of which he is Colonel-in-Chief.*
Opposite above right *Wearing mess dress of the Royal Regiment of Wales.*
Opposite below left *The Prince wearing his uniform as Colonel-in-Chief of the 2nd King Edward VII Own Gurkhas.*
Opposite below right *The Prince wearing the uniform of Air Commodore RAF, which honorary rank he holds.*

Below *The Prince, dressed in tropical naval uniform, during his West African tour in 1977.*

Opposite *Prince Charles is Colonel-in-Chief of the Parachute Regiment. He earned the right to wear the famous 'red beret' by qualifying as a parachutist himself.*

Life in Public

In 1958, the Queen announced that she had created Prince Charles the Prince of Wales, which automatically made him a member of the Order of the Garter. The appointments to this Order, which is the oldest in Chivalry, are traditionally announced on St George's Day, the 23rd April. The Prince was officially installed as a Member of the Order in June 1968 at Windsor Castle.

On 1st July 1968, the Prince knelt before his mother at Caernarvon Castle to be invested as the twenty-first Prince of Wales, following the age-old ceremony which was conducted partly in English and partly in Welsh. His appointment as a Knight of the Garter made him a Member of the second rank of Chivalry, the Order of the Bath, and he was installed at a ceremony in London while serving with the Royal Navy.

After leaving the Royal Navy in 1976, he devoted his energies to organising the celebrations for his mother's Jubilee in 1977. He was the President of the Appeal.

An inveterate traveller, the Prince has journeyed all over the world. He enjoys his trips, entering into all activities with enthusiasm, and adapting to many different situations with a keen perception. His general knowledge amazes his listeners. Prince Charles is one who can mix with kings and commoners alike with consummate ease, whether it be in a formal ceremony or while dancing a samba in Rio de Janeiro.

Ceremonies

Opposite *The Prince, with his grandmother, Queen Elizabeth, the Queen Mother, who is herself a Lady of the Garter, driving away after a ceremony at Windsor Castle.*
Above *Prince Charles after his installation as a Knight of the Garter at Windsor Castle in June 1968. When the Queen bestowed on her son the title of Prince of Wales in 1958, he automatically became a Knight of the Garter, but he was not installed until ten years later. He is also a Knight of the Thistle.*
Above right *At Caernarvon Castle on 1st July 1968, the Prince kneels before his mother who invests him as the twenty-first Prince of Wales.*
Right *After the Investiture ceremony, the Prince and his parents listen to the speeches in Welsh. Later Prince Charles toured the principality.*

Left *Prince Charles making a speech after being given the Freedom of the City of London at a ceremony in 1971. He also holds the titles of Freeman of Cardiff, awarded in 1969, and Freeman of New Windsor, awarded in 1970.*
Below *Prince Charles travels with his great uncle, the late Lord Louis Mountbatten from the Order of the Bath ceremony.*
Opposite *On 28th May 1975, while serving on HMS* Hermes, *the Prince left New Brunswick in Canada where he was training with the Royal Canadian Air Force on a month's helicopter course. He returned to London where the Queen installed him as Great Master of the Order of the Bath. The Order, which ranks second only to the Garter among England's Orders of Knighthood, was originated in the reign of George I. It is said that the King bathed his knights as a token of purity. The Order was founded in 1725 and Prince Charles' installation took place on the two-hundred-and-fiftieth anniversary.*

Left *Prince Charles smiles as his parents, Queen Elizabeth II and Prince Philip, leave St Paul's Cathedral after attending the celebratory service for the Queen's Jubilee in June 1977. The Prince, in the uniform of Colonel-in-Chief of the Welsh Guards, rode to St Paul's on horseback behind his parents' ceremonial coach. His role in the Jubilee celebrations began as soon as he left the Royal Navy. He launched a Silver Jubilee Fund which raised over fifteen million pounds for youth projects. It was his appointment as President of the Appeal that helped to make it such a success.*

Below *After the Jubilee Service and luncheon, Prince Charles stands with his family on the balcony of Buckingham Palace to acknowledge the cheers of the thousands who had gathered in the Mall and around the Palace.*

Right *Prince Charles, the centre of a delighted crowd, during one of his many Jubilee walkabouts.*

Opposite *Prince Charles taking the salute at the Combined Cavalry Old Comrades Parade in Hyde Park.*

Trips abroad

Below *In February 1971, the Prince went on a safari holiday in Kenya with Princess Anne. Here he is conferring with his guides before going on a trek north of Nairobi.*

Below *On his two-week stay in Kenya, the Prince was able to track and photograph many game animals. He spent four days on camel safari in a region inhabited by spear-carrying nomadic tribes. The party camped in the wild and cooked over open fires. The Prince especially enjoyed being able to walk freely about the hot, dry bushland of Africa and to suddenly come upon a wild animal. On his return he remarked that it was 'certainly one of the best things I have done'.*
Opposite *In July 1973, wearing the uniform of Colonel-in-Chief of the Royal Regiment of Wales, the Prince represented the Queen at the Independence Day Celebrations in Nassau. Here he is dancing with the Prime Minister's wife.*

Opposite *The Prince visited the colony of Hong Kong in March 1979. Here he is seen in RAF uniform, painting one of the famous Chinese dragons which so often appear in processions.*
Left *In naval uniform, the Prince descends the ship's gangway at the start of his visit to the colony.*
Below *The Prince talking with a group of athletes in Hong Kong.*

Left *In October 1978, Prince Charles paid an official visit to Yugoslavia. Here he is talking to colourfully dressed people at a reception.*
Below *At the Calgary Stampede in Alberta with his brother, Prince Andrew, and three pretty girls.*
Opposite *On his five-day visit to Alberta in July 1977, the Prince enjoys a buggy ride.*

Opposite *On his visit to Alberta in July 1977, the Prince witnessed the re-enactment of the signing of a peace treaty with the Indians, which took place a hundred years earlier. He was made an honorary chief and given the name Red Crow.*
Right *Prince Charles in Australia sports one of the well-known hats with corks to keep away the flies.*
Below *In March 1979, the Prince paid a visit to a sheep station at Meekatharra in Western Australia. He toured the vast sheep station on horseback.*

Below *Prince Charles accompanies his aunt, Princess Margaret, to Royal Ascot.*

Opposite *Driving a pair at Smith's Lawn, Windsor Great Park. The Prince is wearing a morning suit and a topper.*

Right *In steel helmet and overalls, the Prince makes an inspection of a mine on a tour of the Duchy of Cornwall in 1970.*
Below *The Prince wearing a kilt on an official visit to Scotland.*
Opposite above *The Prince 'measuring' the size of the catch with the crew of a fishing vessel in Scotland.*
Opposite below *On one of the Royal Family's 'walkabouts', the Prince passes a smiling crowd of people who have gathered to welcome him.*

Prince Charles has always been keen on flying, and in the summer of 1979 he enjoyed over an hour in the air in the rear seat of a pre-war Tiger Moth. After the trip, for part of which he took the controls, the Prince, dressed in traditional leather jacket and silk scarf, chatted to newsmen and photographers.

Private Life

The Prince has said that he is happiest when he is with his family and able to share with them many interests and pleasures. His grandmother, with whom he has a special bond, encouraged in him a love of fishing and he often enjoys the quiet relaxation of Scottish streams and Hampshire rivers. He is also an accomplished musician, learning to play the trumpet and the 'cello. He admits to a liking for all kinds of music, from classical to pop, and particularly tunes with good dancing rhythms.

Prince Charles made his debut in the game of polo in 1969, scoring a goal in his first match. He is now one of the best polo players in England. He is a fine marksman, sailor, horseman and archer and has recently taken up the exciting sport of wind-surfing. He is an accomplished skier, winning a gold medal in Switzerland in 1963 in his first skiing test.

Like any young man, he likes the company of girls and is often pictured with a pretty one at his side.

The photographers and newspapers tend to portray him as the polo-playing pleasure-loving prince; but while he certainly enjoys his leisure time, he works extremely hard to earn it. Prince Charles is a man of many parts, and one who is ever ready to widen his horizons by tackling something new. He usually does well at whatever he tries.

Sporting life

Opposite *The Prince playing polo, one of his favourite sports, at Deauville in France.*
Left *The Prince gives his deserving pony a drink between chukkas at a polo match.*
Below *Prince Charles, captain of the Windsor Park Polo Team, sharing with the other members the triumph of winning the tournament in June 1974.*

Above *An excellent shot, the Prince is shown here in action at Bisley.*
Left *The Prince, a keen yachtsman, enjoying a sail. He has frequently participated in the annual Cowes Week events.*
Above right *To 'get away from it all' during an Australian trip, Prince Charles went on a fishing expedition. To his delight he landed an almost record-sized blue marlin.*
Right *The Prince indulging in one of his latest sports – wind-surfing. It is difficult to master but he does not seem to mind how many times he falls in the water!*

Opposite *An expert skier, the Prince on holiday in the snow prepares for his descent.*
Above *At a Game Fair in Wales, he masters the art of archery.*
Left *A first class shot, Prince Charles practising clay pigeon shooting at the Triathlon Event at the Royal Windsor Horse Show.*

Below *The Prince taking a breather after a polo match and discussing play with his great-uncle, the late Lord Louis Mountbatten, himself an expert in the game.*

Opposite *Prince Charles watching a polo match at Windsor.*

Family life

Overleaf *The twenty-four-year-old prince doing a 'highland fling' at Balmoral with his cousin, Lady Sarah Armstrong-Jones, then aged eight. He is wearing a kilt of Balmoral tartan.*

Below *Prince Charles acting as an official at the Badminton Horse Trials.*

Opposite *A keen motorist, Prince Charles climbs into his blue convertible Aston Martin V8 after a polo match.*

Below *The Prince relaxing at the Badminton Horse Trials with the Queen and Prince Andrew.*

Opposite above *Wearing the uniform of Naval Commander, Prince Charles and Prince Philip attend Lord Louis Mountbatten's funeral.*

Opposite below *Prince Charles reading the Lesson at the funeral service for Lord Louis Mountbatten, which was held in Westminster Abbey.*

Left *The drawing-room at Chevening House in Kent, the private home of the Prince of Wales. The house was bequeathed to him by Lord Stanhope.*
Below *The front of the house, a beautiful seventeenth century mansion designed by Inigo Jones, and standing in 3,000 acres of land.*
Opposite *Another view of the house showing the colourful gardens which surround it.*

Left *A surprise kiss for the Prince during an early morning swim in Perth, Australia in 1979. Miss Priest, a bikini-clad model admitted 'I couldn't resist him'. So there are some compensations for being a Prince!*
Opposite *The Prince, dressed for polo, with Lady Sarah Spencer, one of the many girls with whom he has been photographed.*
Overleaf *Prince Charles, in morning suit and top hat, takes Davina Sheffield for a drive in Windsor Great Park.*

1513 NT

Prince Charles relaxes at polo in the company of a girlfriend.

Acknowledgements

The publishers would like to thank the following for their help in supplying photographs for this book.

All photographs are by courtesy of Camera Press Limited except those listed below:

Fox Photos Limited: page 40.

Keystone Press Agency Limited: page 5 (bottom), page 11 (top right), page 16 (bottom), page 24 (bottom), page 37 (bottom), page 57.

Popperfoto: page 11 (left and bottom), page 12, page 17, page 24 (top), pages 29–30.

The Press Association Limited: page 25.

Syndication International Limited: page 16 (top).

Published 1980 by Purnell Books
Berkshire House, Queen Street, Maidenhead, Berkshire
Designed and produced for Purnell Books by
Intercontinental Book Productions

SBN 361 04842 4

Printed in Hong Kong